CHINESE
HOROSCOPES
FOR
LOVERS

The Tiger

LORI REID

illustrated by
PAUL COLLICUTT

ELEMENT BOOKS

Shaftesbury, Dorset • Rockport, Massachusetts • Brisbane, Queensland

First published in Great Britain in 1996 by

ELEMENT BOOKS LIMITED

Shaftesbury, Dorset SP7 8BP

Published in the USA in 1996 by

ELEMENT BOOKS, INC.

PO Box 830, Rockport, MA 01966

Published in Australia in 1996 by

ELEMENT BOOKS LIMITED

for JACARANDA WILEY LIMITED

33 Park Road, Milton, Brisbane 4064

Designed and created by

THE BRIDGEWATER BOOK COMPANY

Art directed by *Peter Bridgewater*

Designed by *Angela Neal*

Picture research by *Vanessa Fletcher*

Edited by *Gillian Delaforce*

Printed and bound in Great Britain by

BPC Paulton Books Ltd

British Library Cataloguing in Publication data available

Library of Congress Cataloging in Publication data available

ISBN 1-85230-763-3

Contents

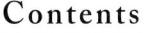

虎

8

*Why are
some people
lucky in
love and
others not?*

Chinese Astrology

SOME PEOPLE fall in love and, as the fairy tales go, live happily ever after. Others fall in love – again and again, make the same mistakes every time and never form a lasting relationship. Most of us come between these two extremes,

and some people form remarkably successful unions while others make spectacular disasters of their personal lives. Why are some people lucky in love while others have the odds stacked against them?

ANIMAL NAMES
According to the philosophy of the Far East, luck has very little to do with it. The answer, the philosophers say, lies with 'the Animal that hides in our hearts'. This Animal, of which there are 12, forms part of the complex art of Chinese Astrology. Each year of a 12-year cycle is attributed an Animal sign, whose characteristics are said to influence worldly events as well as the personality and fate of each living thing that comes under its dominion. The 12 Animals run in sequence, beginning with the Rat and followed by the Ox, Tiger, Rabbit, Dragon, Snake, Horse, Sheep, Monkey, Rooster, Dog and last, but not least, the Pig. Being born in the Year of the Ox, for example, is simply a way of describing what you're like, physically and psychologically. And this is quite different from someone who, for instance, is born in the Year of the Snake.

CHINESE
ASTROLOGY

虎

9

*The 12
Animals
of Chinese
Astrology.*

RELATIONSHIPS

These Animal names are merely the tip of the ice-
berg, considering the complexity of the whole
subject. Yet such are the richness and wisdom of Chinese
Astrology that understanding the principles behind the year in
which you were born will give you powerful insights into your
own personality. The system is very specific about which Animals
are compatible and which are antagonistic and this tells us
whether our relationships will be successful. Marriages are made
in heaven, so the saying goes. The heavens, according to Chinese
beliefs, can point the way. The rest is up to us.

虎

10

Year Chart and Birth Dates

UNLIKE THE WESTERN CALENDAR, which is based on the Sun, the Oriental year is based on the movement of the Moon, which means that New Year's Day does not fall on a fixed date. This Year Chart, taken from the Chinese Perpetual Calendar, lists the dates on which each year begins and ends together with its Animal ruler for the year. In addition, the Chinese believe that the tangible world is composed of 5 elements, each slightly adapting the characteristics of the Animal signs. These elemental influences are also given here. Finally, the aspect, that is whether the year is characteristically Yin (-) or Yang (+), is also listed.

The Western calendar is based on the Sun; the Oriental on the Moon.

YIN AND YANG

Yin and Yang are the terms given to the dynamic complementary forces that keep the universe in balance and which are the central principles behind life. Yin is all that is considered negative, passive, feminine, night, the Moon, while Yang is considered positive, active, masculine, day, the Sun.

YEAR CHART AND BIRTH DATES

Year	From – To	Animal sign	Element	Aspect	
1900	31 Jan 1900 – 18 Feb 1901	Rat	Metal	Yang	+
1901	19 Feb 1901 – 7 Feb 1902	Ox	Metal	Yin	–
1902	8 Feb 1902 – 28 Jan 1903	Tiger	Water	Yang	+
1903	29 Jan 1903 – 15 Feb 1904	Rabbit	Water	Yin	–
1904	16 Feb 1904 – 3 Feb 1905	Dragon	Wood	Yang	+
1905	4 Feb 1905 – 24 Jan 1906	Snake	Wood	Yin	–
1906	25 Jan 1906 – 12 Feb 1907	Horse	Fire	Yang	+
1907	13 Feb 1907 – 1 Feb 1908	Sheep	Fire	Yin	–
1908	2 Feb 1908 – 21 Jan 1909	Monkey	Earth	Yang	+
1909	22 Jan 1909 – 9 Feb 1910	Rooster	Earth	Yin	–
1910	10 Feb 1910 – 29 Jan 1911	Dog	Metal	Yang	+
1911	30 Jan 1911 – 17 Feb 1912	Pig	Metal	Yin	–
1912	18 Feb 1912 – 5 Feb 1913	Rat	Water	Yang	+
1913	6 Feb 1913 – 25 Jan 1914	Ox	Water	Yin	–
1914	26 Jan 1914 – 13 Feb 1915	Tiger	Wood	Yang	+
1915	14 Feb 1915 – 2 Feb 1916	Rabbit	Wood	Yin	–
1916	3 Feb 1916 – 22 Jan 1917	Dragon	Fire	Yang	+
1917	23 Jan 1917 – 10 Feb 1918	Snake	Fire	Yin	–
1918	11 Feb 1918 – 31 Jan 1919	Horse	Earth	Yang	+
1919	1 Feb 1919 – 19 Feb 1920	Sheep	Earth	Yin	–
1920	20 Feb 1920 – 7 Feb 1921	Monkey	Metal	Yang	+
1921	8 Feb 1921 – 27 Jan 1922	Rooster	Metal	Yin	–
1922	28 Jan 1922 – 15 Feb 1923	Dog	Water	Yang	+
1923	16 Feb 1923 – 4 Feb 1924	Pig	Water	Yin	–
1924	5 Feb 1924 – 24 Jan 1925	Rat	Wood	Yang	+
1925	25 Jan 1925 – 12 Feb 1926	Ox	Wood	Yin	–
1926	13 Feb 1926 – 1 Feb 1927	Tiger	Fire	Yang	+
1927	2 Feb 1927 – 22 Jan 1928	Rabbit	Fire	Yin	–
1928	23 Jan 1928 – 9 Feb 1929	Dragon	Earth	Yang	+
1929	10 Feb 1929 – 29 Jan 1930	Snake	Earth	Yin	–
1930	30 Jan 1930 – 16 Feb 1931	Horse	Metal	Yang	+
1931	17 Feb 1931 – 5 Feb 1932	Sheep	Metal	Yin	–
1932	6 Feb 1932 – 25 Jan 1933	Monkey	Water	Yang	+
1933	26 Jan 1933 – 13 Feb 1934	Rooster	Water	Yin	–
1934	14 Feb 1934 – 3 Feb 1935	Dog	Wood	Yang	+
1935	4 Feb 1935 – 23 Jan 1936	Pig	Wood	Yin	–

Year	From – To	Animal sign	Element	Aspect
1936	24 Jan 1936 – 10 Feb 1937	Rat	Fire	+ Yang
1937	11 Feb 1937 – 30 Jan 1938	Ox	Fire	– Yin
1938	31 Jan 1938 – 18 Feb 1939	Tiger	Earth	+ Yang
1939	19 Feb 1939 – 7 Feb 1940	Rabbit	Earth	– Yin
1940	8 Feb 1940 – 26 Jan 1941	Dragon	Metal	+ Yang
1941	27 Jan 1941 – 14 Feb 1942	Snake	Metal	– Yin
1942	15 Feb 1942 – 4 Feb 1943	Horse	Water	+ Yang
1943	5 Feb 1943 – 24 Jan 1944	Sheep	Water	– Yin
1944	25 Jan 1944 – 12 Feb 1945	Monkey	Wood	+ Yang
1945	13 Feb 1945 – 1 Feb 1946	Rooster	Wood	– Yin
1946	2 Feb 1946 – 21 Jan 1947	Dog	Fire	+ Yang
1947	22 Jan 1947 – 9 Feb 1948	Pig	Fire	– Yin
1948	10 Feb 1948 – 28 Jan 1949	Rat	Earth	+ Yang
1949	29 Jan 1949 – 16 Feb 1950	Ox	Earth	– Yin
1950	17 Feb 1950 – 5 Feb 1951	Tiger	Metal	+ Yang
1951	6 Feb 1951 – 26 Jan 1952	Rabbit	Metal	– Yin
1952	27 Jan 1952 – 13 Feb 1953	Dragon	Water	+ Yang
1953	14 Feb 1953 – 2 Feb 1954	Snake	Water	– Yin
1954	3 Feb 1954 – 23 Jan 1955	Horse	Wood	+ Yang
1955	24 Jan 1955 – 11 Feb 1956	Sheep	Wood	– Yin
1956	12 Feb 1956 – 30 Jan 1957	Monkey	Fire	+ Yang
1957	31 Jan 1957 – 17 Feb 1958	Rooster	Fire	– Yin
1958	18 Feb 1958 – 7 Feb 1959	Dog	Earth	+ Yang
1959	8 Feb 1959 – 27 Jan 1960	Pig	Earth	– Yin
1960	28 Jan 1960 – 14 Feb 1961	Rat	Metal	+ Yang
1961	15 Feb 1961 – 4 Feb 1962	Ox	Metal	– Yin
1962	5 Feb 1962 – 24 Jan 1963	Tiger	Water	+ Yang
1963	25 Jan 1963 – 12 Feb 1964	Rabbit	Water	– Yin
1964	13 Feb 1964 – 1 Feb 1965	Dragon	Wood	+ Yang
1965	2 Feb 1965 – 20 Jan 1966	Snake	Wood	– Yin
1966	21 Jan 1966 – 8 Feb 1967	Horse	Fire	+ Yang
1967	9 Feb 1967 – 29 Jan 1968	Sheep	Fire	– Yin
1968	30 Jan 1968 – 16 Feb 1969	Monkey	Earth	+ Yang
1969	17 Feb 1969 – 5 Feb 1970	Rooster	Earth	– Yin
1970	6 Feb 1970 – 26 Jan 1971	Dog	Metal	+ Yang
1971	27 Jan 1971 – 15 Jan 1972	Pig	Metal	– Yin

YEAR CHART AND BIRTH DATES

Year	From – To	Animal sign	Element	Aspect	
1972	16 Jan 1972 – 2 Feb 1973	Rat	Water	+	Yang
1973	3 Feb 1973 – 22 Jan 1974	Ox	Water	–	Yin
1974	23 Jan 1974 – 10 Feb 1975	Tiger	Wood	+	Yang
1975	11 Feb 1975 – 30 Jan 1976	Rabbit	Wood	–	Yin
1976	31 Jan 1976 – 17 Feb 1977	Dragon	Fire	+	Yang
1977	18 Feb 1977 – 6 Feb 1978	Snake	Fire	–	Yin
1978	7 Feb 1978 – 27 Jan 1979	Horse	Earth	+	Yang
1979	28 Jan 1979 – 15 Feb 1980	Sheep	Earth	–	Yin
1980	16 Feb 1980 – 4 Feb 1981	Monkey	Metal	+	Yang
1981	5 Feb 1981 – 24 Jan 1982	Rooster	Metal	–	Yin
1982	25 Jan 1982 – 12 Feb 1983	Dog	Water	+	Yang
1983	13 Feb 1983 – 1 Feb 1984	Pig	Water	–	Yin
1984	2 Feb 1984 – 19 Feb 1985	Rat	Wood	+	Yang
1985	20 Feb 1985 – 8 Feb 1986	Ox	Wood	–	Yin
1986	9 Feb 1986 – 28 Jan 1987	Tiger	Fire	+	Yang
1987	29 Jan 1987 – 16 Feb 1988	Rabbit	Fire	–	Yin
1988	17 Feb 1988 – 5 Feb 1989	Dragon	Earth	+	Yang
1989	6 Feb 1989 – 26 Jan 1990	Snake	Earth	–	Yin
1990	27 Jan 1990 – 14 Feb 1991	Horse	Metal	+	Yang
1991	15 Feb 1991 – 3 Feb 1992	Sheep	Metal	–	Yin
1992	4 Feb 1992 – 22 Jan 1993	Monkey	Water	+	Yang
1993	23 Jan 1993 – 9 Feb 1994	Rooster	Water	–	Yin
1994	10 Feb 1994 – 30 Jan 1995	Dog	Wood	+	Yang
1995	31 Jan 1995 – 18 Feb 1996	Pig	Wood	–	Yin
1996	19 Feb 1996 – 7 Feb 1997	Rat	Fire	+	Yang
1997	8 Feb 1997 – 27 Jan 1998	Ox	Fire	–	Yin
1998	28 Jan 1998 – 15 Feb 1999	Tiger	Earth	+	Yang
1999	16 Feb 1999 – 4 Feb 2000	Rabbit	Earth	–	Yin
2000	5 Feb 2000 – 23 Jan 2001	Dragon	Metal	+	Yang
2001	24 Jan 2001 – 11 Feb 2002	Snake	Metal	–	Yin
2002	12 Feb 2002 – 31 Jan 2003	Horse	Water	+	Yang
2003	1 Feb 2003 – 21 Jan 2004	Sheep	Water	–	Yin
2004	22 Jan 2004 – 8 Feb 2005	Monkey	Wood	+	Yang
2005	9 Feb 2005 – 28 Jan 2006	Rooster	Wood	–	Yin
2006	29 Jan 2006 – 17 Feb 2007	Dog	Fire	+	Yang
2007	18 Feb 2007 – 9 Feb 2008	Pig	Fire	–	Yin

Introducing the Animals

THE RAT   ♥ ♥ ♥ DRAGON, MONKEY   ✖ HORSE

Outwardly cool, Rats are passionate lovers with depths of feeling that others don't often recognize. Rats are very self-controlled.

THE OX   ♥ ♥ ♥ SNAKE, ROOSTER   ✖ SHEEP

Not necessarily the most romantic of the signs, Ox people make steadfast lovers as well as faithful, affectionate partners.

THE TIGER   ♥ ♥ ♥ HORSE, DOG   ✖ MONKEY

Passionate and sensual, Tigers are exciting lovers. Flirty when young, once committed they make stable partners and keep their sexual allure.

THE RABBIT   ♥ ♥ ♥ SHEEP, PIG   ✖ ROOSTER

Gentle, emotional and sentimental, Rabbits make sensitive lovers. They are shrewd and seek a partner who offers security.

THE DRAGON   ♥ ♥ ♥ RAT, MONKEY   ✖ DOG

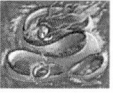

Dragon folk get as much stimulation from mind-touch as they do through sex. A partner on the same wave-length is essential.

THE SNAKE   ♥ ♥ ♥ OX, ROOSTER   ✖ PIG

Deeply passionate, strongly sexed but not aggressive snakes are attracted to elegant, refined partners. But they are deeply jealous and possessive.

虎

15

♥ ♥ ♥ *COMPATIBLE*　　✖ *INCOMPATIBLE*

HE HORSE	♥ ♥ ♥ TIGER, DOG	✖ RAT

For horse-born folk love is blind. In losing their hearts, they lose their heads and make several mistakes before finding the right partner.

HE SHEEP	♥ ♥ ♥ RABBIT, PIG	✖ OX

Sheep-born people are made for marriage. Domesticated home-lovers, they find emotional satisfaction with a partner who provides security.

HE MONKEY	♥ ♥ ♥ DRAGON, RAT	✖ TIGER

Clever and witty, Monkeys need partners who will keep them stimulated. Forget the 9 to 5 routine, these people need *pizzazz*.

HE ROOSTER	♥ ♥ ♥ OX, SNAKE	✖ RABBIT

The Rooster's stylish good looks guarantee they will attract many suitors. They are level-headed and approach relationships coolly.

HE DOG	♥ ♥ ♥ TIGER, HORSE	✖ DRAGON

A loving, stable relationship is an essential component in the lives of Dogs. Once they have found their mate, they remain faithful for life.

HE PIG	♥ ♥ ♥ RABBIT, SHEEP	✖ SNAKE

These are sensual hedonists who enjoy lingering love-making between satin sheets. Caviar and champagne go down very nicely too.

虎

16

The Tiger Personality

THE LEAST snobbish member of the Chinese Animals, you're not impressed by power or money. Yet you're colourful, dynamic and attractive. Your enthusiasm and optimism guarantee you the approval you constantly seek. The Chinese say a Tiger in the house is the best insurance against fire, theft and evil spirits, perhaps because Tigers are lucky and fight bravely. Like all felines you always land on your feet but your indomitable energy means that you systematically burn the candle at both ends.

TIGER FACTS

Third in order ★ *Chinese name – Hu* ★ *Sign of courage*
★ *Hour – 3AM-4. 59AM* ★ *Month – February* ★
★ *Western counterpart – Aquarius* ★

CHARACTERISTICS

♥ *Courage* ♥ *Enthusiasm* ♥ *Boldness* ♥ *Sociability*
♥ *Energy* ♥ *Optimism*

✘ *Volatility* ✘ *Impulsiveness* ✘ *Impatience*
✘ *Hot-headedness* ✘ *Vanity* ✘ *Disobedience*

虎

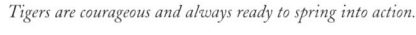

Tigers are courageous and always ready to spring into action.

FREEDOM FIGHTER

It's also true that you're incorrigibly competitive – you simply can't pass up a challenge when honour is at stake, particularly if it comes to defending those you love. There is something noble about the way you take up arms, especially when it means fighting for justice and freedom. Since Tigers are unpredictable, people would be unwise to underestimate your reactions. You may appear cool, but you have the Big Cat's instincts to pounce at a moment's warning.

TIGER TACTICS

Your intelligence is evident and you are alert and far-sighted. You have your finger on the pulse and, as in a game of chess, are always several moves ahead. A good strategist and tactician, there's often the hint of a hidden agenda in your dealings.

Tiger folk are also good tacticians.

Your Hour of Birth

WHILE YOUR YEAR OF BIRTH describes your fundamental character, the Animal governing the actual hour in which you were born describes your outer temperament, how people see you or the picture you present to the outside world. Note that each Animal rules over two consecutive hours. Also note that these are GMT standard times and that adjustments need to be made if you were born during Summer or daylight saving time.

11PM – 12.59AM ★ RAT
Pleasant, sociable, easy to get on with. An active, confident, busy person – and a bit of a busybody to boot.

1AM – 2.59AM ★ OX
Level-headed and down-to-earth, you come across as knowledgeable and reliable – sometimes, though, a bit biased.

3AM – 4.59AM ★ TIGER
Enthusiastic and self-assured, people see you as a strong and positive personality – at times a little over-exuberant.

5AM – 6.59AM ★ RABBIT
You're sensitive and shy and don't project your real self to the world. You feel you have to put on an act to please others.

7AM – 8.59AM ★ DRAGON
Independent and interesting, you present a picture of someone who is quite out of the ordinary.

9AM – 10.59AM ★ SNAKE
You can be a bit difficult to fathom and, because you appear so controlled, people either take to you instantly, or not at all.

11AM – 12.59PM ★ HORSE

Open, cheerful and happy-go-lucky is the picture you always put across to others. You're an extrovert and it generally shows.

1PM – 2.59PM ★ SHEEP

Your unassuming nature won't allow you to foist yourself upon others so people see you as quiet and retiring – but eminently sensible, though.

3PM – 4.59PM ★ MONKEY

Lively and talkative, that twinkle in your eye will guarantee you make friends wherever you go.

5PM – 6.59PM ★ ROOSTER

There's something rather stylish in your approach that gives people an impression of elegance and glamour. But you don't suffer fools gladly.

7PM – 8.59PM ★ DOG

Some people see you as steady and reliable, others as quiet and graceful and others still as dull and unimaginative. It all depends who you're with at the time.

9PM – 10.59PM ★ PIG

Your laid-back manner conceals a depth of interest and intelligence that doesn't always come through at first glance.

Your hour of birth describes your outer temperament.

虎

20

The Tiger Lover

Tigers are made for love and love-making. They're not happy on their own and need a loving partner to share their lives with. Bold as you may be, the thought of enforced loneliness can make you fairly buckle at the knees. Interestingly, the thought of capture and restriction can equally distress you, for you're a born hunter and need the thrill of the chase.

BEING A TIGER MAKES YOU an attractive creature, passionate and strong. As a lover, you're romantic and ardently sexy. Spontaneous in your desires, you're flirtatious and never quite lose that spark of excitability. And, because you have the unpredictability of a jungle cat, you carry that frisson of excitement around you, that hint of danger that is so irresistible. In too static a

Tigers are flirtatious but fear entrapment.

relationship, you're likely to start pacing like a caged animal, and restlessness and curiosity could get the better of you. It's this that has earned you the reputation for not being the most faithful of the Chinese Animals.

The Kiss
GUSTAV KLIMT 1862–1918

RUN FOR YOUR MONEY

A partner who has his or her head screwed on will give you a good run for your money and keep you guessing just enough to maintain your interest. Besides, bold and fearless you may be, but you draw a great deal of your strength from your family, and from the bonds of a loving union. Perhaps this is why so many Tigers marry young.

LIFE WITH A TIGER

Once committed, you should watch your assertive nature since you tend to dominate your relationships. Also, try not to upset your partner with your outspoken comments. But these are minor faults in comparison to the benefits you bring to a relationship: your warmth and generosity of spirit, that old-fashioned insistence on courteousness, huge appetite for life and spontaneous enjoyment of sex that brings the tingle factor to your love-making.

*Kitchen
Gods*
20TH
CENTURY
PRINT

虎

22

In Your Element

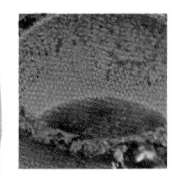

ALTHOUGH YOUR SIGN recurs every 12 years, each generation is slightly modified by one of 5 elements. If you were born under the Metal influence your character, emotions and behaviour would show significant variation from an individual born under one of the other elements. Check the Year Chart for your ruling element and discover what effect it has upon you.

THE METAL TIGER ⋆ 1950

The most outgoing of the element variations, you like to be different and to stand out in a crowd. Metal Tigers and success go together. With your assertive nature and competitive spirit, you fix your sights firmly on the top and are determined to get there.

THE WATER TIGER ⋆ 1902 AND 1962

Although the Tiger fire and passion are still part of your birthright, being born under the Water influence makes you calmer and more placid than other fellow cats. Your ability to take people's feelings and ideas on board makes you reasonable and understanding. You have excellent insight and strong powers of intuition.

THE WOOD TIGER ★ 1914 AND 1974

Better able to work as part of a team, you don't feel that tremendous urge to take charge or to dominate the scene that other elemental Tigers might. Your warmth, generosity and thoroughly agreeable nature ensure that you are popular with your friends. Beware volatile interests and a short attention span.

THE FIRE TIGER ★ 1926 AND 1986

Colourful, active and dramatic, you blaze with passion, enthusiasm, vitality and spunk. You have in-born powers of leadership and a natural ability to inspire people with enthusiasm. With your charismatic presence and persuasive tongue, who could resist following you to the ends of the earth?

THE EARTH TIGER ★ 1938 AND 1998

Generally more realistic, practical and down-to-earth than most other Tigers, you tend not to get swept away quite so readily by your own enthusiasm and excitement. A steadier approach to life, together with the ability to apply yourself for longer periods, brings success through sustained and concentrated efforts.

虎

24

*Rencontre
du Soir
(detail)*
THEOPHILE-
ALEXANDRE
STEINLEN
1859–1923

*Some
relationships
are more
star-tipped
than others.*

Partners in Love

THE CHINESE are very definite about which animals are compatible with each other and which are antagonistic. So find out if you're truly suited to your partner.

TIGER + RAT ★
Expect some dramatic clashes of temperament. Lots of friendship but little true passion.

TIGER + OX ★
Chinese say this is one of the worst matches possible, but you are drawn to each other, nevertheless.

TIGER + TIGER ★
With two such dominant, individualistic creatures, there are bound to be fireworks.

TIGER + RABBIT ★
You're good for each other.

TIGER + DRAGON ★
A gutsy combination with plenty of sparks to fuel the passions.

TIGER + SNAKE ★
Different outlook, different lifestyles and different objectives all suggest little meeting of minds.

TIGER + HORSE ★
Plenty of high jinks in this high-octane relationship ensure an exciting life together.

TIGER + SHEEP ★
Lots of respect but too much treading on eggshells for comfort.

LOVE PARTNERS AT A GLANCE

Tiger with:	Tips on Togetherness	Compatibility
Rat	learn to compromise	♥♥
Ox	a clash of temperaments	♥
Tiger	too much jostling for the upper hand	♥♥
Rabbit	your differences weld you together	♥♥♥
Dragon	a dynamic duo!	♥♥♥
Snake	odds against	♥
Horse	hot and spicy	♥♥♥♥
Sheep	work, yes – marriage, no	♥♥
Monkey	deeply frustrating	♥
Rooster	talk or walk	♥♥
Dog	solid!	♥♥♥♥
Pig	good humour keeps you smiling thro'	♥♥♥

COMPATIBILITY RATINGS:
♥ *conflict* ♥♥ *work at it* ♥♥♥ *strong sexual attraction* ♥♥♥♥ *heavenly!*

TIGER + MONKEY ★
You're likely to drive each other up the wall!

Eiaha chipa
PAUL GAUGUIN 1848-1903

TIGER + ROOSTER ★
Misunderstandings create problems.

TIGER + DOG ★
Mutual respect and admiration make this a solid union and a winning team.

TIGER + PIG ★
Friendship, shared interests, and a good sense of humour bode well for your union.

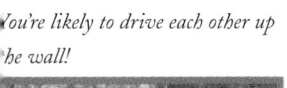

Paolo and Francesca (detail)
ANSELM
FEUERBACH

Hot Dates

IF YOU'RE DATING someone for the first time, taking your partner out for a special occasion or simply wanting to re-ignite that flame of passion between you, it helps to understand what would please that person most.

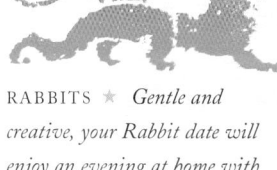

RATS ★ *Wine and dine him or take her to a party. Do something on impulse… go to the races or take a flight in a hot air balloon.*

OXEN ★ *Go for a drive in the country and drop in on a stately home. Visit an art gallery or antique shops. Then have an intimate dinner à deux.*

'So glad to see you…'
COCA-COLA 1945

TIGERS ★ *Tigers thrive on excitement so go clay-pigeon shooting, Formula One racing or challenge each other to a Quasar dual. A date at the theatre will put stars in your Tiger's eyes.*

RABBITS ★ *Gentle and creative, your Rabbit date will enjoy an evening at home with some take-away food and a romantic video. Play some seductive jazz and snuggle up.*

DRAGONS ★ *Mystery and magic will thrill your Dragon date. Take in a son et lumière show or go to a carnival. Or drive to the coast and sink your toes in the sand as the sun sets.*

SNAKES ★ *Don't do anything too active – these creatures like to take life sloooowly. Hire a row-boat for a long, lazy ride down the river. Give a soothing massage, then glide into a sensual jacuzzi together.*

虎

27

The Carnival
GASTON-DOIN 19/20TH CENTURY

HORSES ★ *Your zany Horse gets easily bored. Take her on a mind-spinning tour of the local attractions. Surprise him with tickets to a musical show. Whatever you do, keep them guessing.*

SHEEP ★ *These folk adore the Arts so visit a museum, gallery or poetry recital. Go to a concert, the ballet, or the opera.*

MONKEYS ★ *The fantastical appeals to this partner, so go to a fancy-dress party or a masked ball, a laser light show or a sci-fi movie.*

ROOSTERS ★ *Grand gestures will impress your Rooster. Escort her to a film première or him to a formal engagement. Dressing up will place this date in seventh heaven.*

DOGS ★ *A cosy dinner will please this most unassuming of partners more than any social occasion. Chatting and story telling will ensure a close understanding.*

PIGS ★ *Arrange a slap-up meal or a lively party, or cruise through the shopping mall. Shopping is one of this partner's favourite hobbies!*

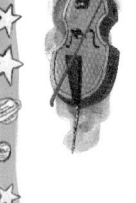

28

Detail from
Chinese
Marriage
Ceremony
CHINESE
PAINTING

Year of Commitment

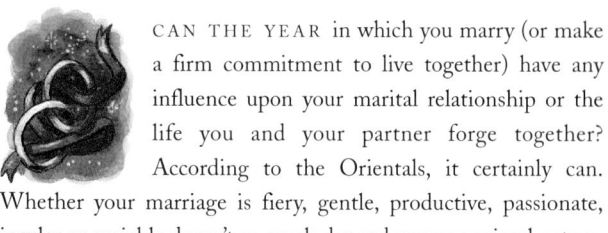

CAN THE YEAR in which you marry (or make a firm commitment to live together) have any influence upon your marital relationship or the life you and your partner forge together? According to the Orientals, it certainly can. Whether your marriage is fiery, gentle, productive, passionate, insular or sociable doesn't so much depend on your animal nature, as on the nature of the Animal in whose year you tied the knot.

IF YOU MARRY IN A YEAR OF THE...

RAT ★ *your marriage should succeed because ventures starting now attract long-term success. Materially, you won't want and life is full of friendship.*

Marriage Feast
CHINESE PAINTING

OX ★ *your relationship will be solid and tastes conventional. Diligence will be recognized and you'll be well respected.*

TIGER ★ *you'll need plenty of humour to ride out the storms. Marrying in the Year of the Tiger is not auspicious.*

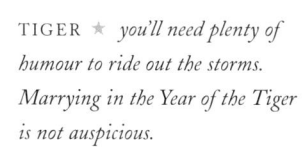

RABBIT ★ *you're wedded under the emblem of lovers. It's auspicious for a happy, carefree relationship, as neither partner wants to rock the boat.*

DRAGON ★ *you're blessed. This year is highly auspicious for luck, happiness and success.*

NAKE ★ *it's good for*
mance but sexual
tanglements are rife. Your
lationship may seem languid,
ut passions run deep.

ORSE ★ *chances are you*
ecided to marry on the spur of
e moment as the Horse year
ncourages impetuous behaviour.
Marriage now may be volatile.

HEEP ★ *your family and home*
re blessed but watch domestic
ending. Money is very easily
ittered away.

Marriage Ceremony
CHINESE PAINTING

MONKEY ★ *married life could*
be unconventional. As plans
go awry your lives could be full
of surprises.

ROOSTER ★ *drama*
characterizes your married life.
Your household will run like
clockwork, but bickering could
strain your relationship.

DOG ★ *it's a truly fortunate*
year and you can expect domestic
joy. Prepare for a large family as
the Dog is the sign of fertility!

PIG ★ *it's highly auspicious and*
there'll be plenty of fun. Watch out
for indulgence and excess.

Marriage Ceremony (detail)
CHINESE PAINTING

Detail from
Chinese
Marriage
Ceremony
CHINESE
PAINTING

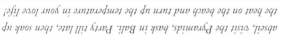

TYPICAL TIGER PLEASURES

COLOUR PREFERENCES ✳ Mid green

Cat's eye

Ruby (rough)

GEMS AND STONES ✳ Ruby, diamond, cat's eye

SUITABLE GIFTS ✳ Crime novel, mah jong set, exotic cookbook, gliding lesson, travel guides, manicure set (to sharpen those claws!)

HOBBIES AND PASTIMES ✳ Action sports, amateur dramatics, noisy parties, the latest fashions, bridge and chess, adventure films, detective stories, photography

HOLIDAY PREFERENCES

Tigers need to feel the edge of danger. Never one to stay at home, you need a holiday packed with adventure. Drive to the outback; go overland to the Far East. Shoot the white rapids, abseil, visit the Pyramids, bask in Bali. Party till late, then soak up the heat on the beach and turn up the temperature in your love life!

Verona, Italy

COUNTRIES LINKED WITH THE TIGER ✳ Italy, France, Ecuador

The Tiger Parent

TIGER PARENTS, like their feline counterparts, are fierce protectors of their young, and you would probably lay down your life to defend your little ones. You're a warm, affectionate parent, lavishing your brood with treats. Often you are playful as a kitten, joining in family games and enjoying your children's company. But there are times when, like all Big Cats, you roar with rage if one of your offspring has gone too far. Open-minded you may be, but you will not tolerate bad manners or rebellious behaviour.

31

Tigers make caring and devoted parents.

EDUCATION

You're a staunch believer in a good education for your children. When they're little you tell them tales about your own childhood, hoping to impart some wisdom and be the best role model going.

THE TIGER HABITAT

As a Tiger, you like to be different, and this applies to your home, for it's here that your original flair can be seen at its best. It may not be bang up-to-date but you have a knack of creating atmosphere with colour and light. Never afraid to experiment, your bold spirit of adventure is reflected in your décor. Your love of travel will be in evidence with treasures from the far-flung places you've visited: Shaker tablecloths, Tibetan prayer mats, African carvings. And there are all those knick-knacks you've picked up for a song with your keen eye for a bargain! New ideas and designs are blended with truly inimitable style.

Animal Babies

FOR SOME parents, their children's personalitie harmonize perfectly with their own. Others fin that no matter how much they may love the offspring they're just not on the same wavelength Our children arrive with their characters alread well formed and, according to Chinese philosophy, shaped by th influence of their Animal Year. So you should be mindful of the yea in which you conceive.

BABIES BORN IN THE YEAR OF THE...

RAT ★ *love being cuddled. They keep on the go – so give them plenty of rest. Later they enjoy collecting things.*

OX ★ *are placid, solid and independent. If not left to their own devices they sulk.*

TIGER ★ *are happy and endearing. As children, they have irrepressible energy. Boys are sporty and girls tom-boys.*

RABBIT ★ *are sensitive and strongly bonded to their mother. They need stability to thrive.*

DRAGON ★ *are independent and imaginative from the start. Encourage any interest that will allow their talents to flourish.*

SNAKE ★ *have great charm. They are slow starters so may nee help with school work. Teach ther to express feelings.*

One Hundred Children Scroll
ANON, MING PERIOD

HORSE ★ *will burble away contentedly for hours. Talking starts early and they excel in languages.*

SHEEP ★ *are placid, well-behaved and respectful. They are family-oriented and never stray too far from home.*

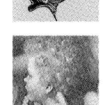

MONKEY ★ *take an insatiable interest in everything. With agile minds they're quick to learn. They're good-humoured but mischievous!*

ROOSTER ★ *are sociable. Bright and vivacious, their strong adventurous streak best shows itself on a sports field.*

DOG ★ *are cute and cuddly. Easily pleased, they are content just pottering around the house amusing themselves for hours. Common sense is their greatest virtue.*

PIG ★ *are affectionate and friendly. Well-balanced, self-confident children, they're happy-go-lucky and laid-back. They are popular with friends.*

Health, Wealth and Worldly Affairs

IF HEALTH WERE MEASURED by how one runs a race, you'd be a sprinter because you tackle life in short bursts of energy and then collapse with exhaustion. You should learn to pace yourself in order to keep active longer and prevent early burn-out. The main problems you're likely to encounter are accidents and injuries due to impulsive action, but you're blessed with a resilient constitution and recover quickly from any ill-health.

Tigers may juggle several jobs at once.

Tigers like to be big fish in little ponds, so you work much better at the head of a small team than as chief of a vast corporation. You make a bold, kind leader, concerned about your workforce and able to inspire them with confidence.

CAREER

With your active and alert intelligence, you're a fast learner and able to pick up skills quickly. Like all Tigers, you like a challenge and this, coupled with your restlessness, explains why you tend to change careers more often than other Chinese Animals. Or else you juggle several jobs all at the same time.

虎

*Tigers often take shortcuts, but their gambles
usually pay off.*

FINANCES

Luck plays a large part in your finances. You know you can make money whenever you need it, so dipping into the red doesn't alarm you. Somehow you manage to find a pot of gold just when it seems you're heading for skid row. Tigers may lose a fortune in their time, but will often end up with two, to make up for the initial loss.

FRIENDSHIPS

As a friend, you're warm and generous and have the gift of lifting the spirits of even the gloomiest individual. Should a friend drop by for a needy chat, you'll down tools and offer a ready ear and a broad shoulder to cry on. Few friends could be as supportive, as funny or as genuinely concerned as you.

TIGERS MAKE EXCELLENT:

★ Actors ★ Comedians ★ Musicians ★ Racing drivers ★
★ Chauffeurs ★ Explorers ★ Pilots ★ Artists ★ Writers ★
★ Air hostesses ★ Travel agents ★ Advertising agents ★
★ Lecturers ★ Politicians ★ Missionaries ★ Office managers ★
★ Members of the armed forces ★ Sales personnel ★

虎

East Meets West

COMBINE YOUR Oriental Animal sign with your Western Zodiac birth sign to form a deeper and richer understanding of your character and personality.

ARIES TIGER

★ *Fiery and impetuous, you whizz through life like a tornado, cramming activities into the day. Loving and attractive, you're likely to have several lovers before you settle down.*

TAUREAN TIGER

★ *Steadier than the average Tiger, you can apply yourself practically to all tasks you undertake. Your relationships tend to be stable – without losing a single ounce of that Tiger passion!*

GEMINI TIGER

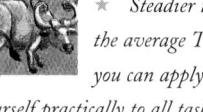

★ *Constantly on the move, variety is the spice of life for you. Being tied to one place and one person for the rest of your life is your worst nightmare.*

CANCERIAN TIGER

★ *Couple the romantic nature of the Crab with the Tiger and see what a hot lover you are! But, underneath you're a tender-hearted puss. A secure home and stable relationship are what you seek.*

LEONINE TIGER

★ *What a scorcher! When lion couples with tiger it makes for a bold, fiery personality. Only a partner as strong as you would capture your interest, otherwise just keep on hunting.*

VIRGO TIGER

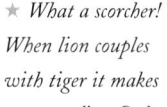

★ *Your natural caution tempers your impetuosity. Practical and hard-working, your high expectations mean you are selective in your relationships.*

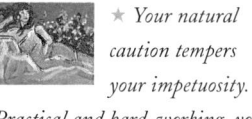

LIBRAN TIGER

★ With your affable nature, charm and drop-dead good looks, you're bound to have an army of potential suitors buzzing around you all the time. The pity of it is, you have such trouble making up your mind!

SCORPIO TIGER

★ Cats have nine lives, and no-one lives them as intensely as a Scorpio-Tiger. Sensual and sultry, you're a hot sexy lover who burns with desire, but if crossed in love, you will seethe with rage and brook no interference until you find revenge.

SAGITTARIAN TIGER

★ Of all the Tigers you are the most far-sighted. You're extroverted and like to experience everything that life has to offer. Your independence is vitally important to you, so you need an understanding partner who won't attempt to clip your wings.

CAPRICORN TIGER

★ You've set your heart on reaching the top. Ambitious, you know that success comes through hard work so you're prepared to put in long hours to achieve the status you believe you deserve. Love and relationships come second.

AQUARIAN TIGER

★ You're a law unto yourself and very unpredictable too. Because you're able to rationalize your feelings, you come across as emotionally cool. Intellectual and idealistic, you get more passionate over a philosophical argument than over a romp in the hay.

PISCEAN TIGER

★ The tender influence of your Piscean nature will moderate your Tiger aggression and hot-headedness, but the fiery passions are still there aplenty. When you set your sights on a partner, you'll use your sharpest insights and cleverest wiles to stake your claim.

虎

FAMOUS TIGERS

General de Gaulle

Agatha Christie

Marilyn Monroe

Karl Marx

Rudolf Nureyev

D D Eisenhower

Ho Chi Minh

★ *Agatha Christie* ★ *Marilyn Monroe* ★ *Rudolf Nureyev* ★
★ *Beethoven* ★ *Dwight D Eisenhower* ★ *Karl Marx* ★
★ *Ho Chi Minh* ★ *Charles de Gaulle* ★ *Louis XIV* ★
★ *Marie Curie* ★ *HM Queen Elizabeth II* ★
★ *HRH The Princess Royal* ★ *Richard Branson* ★
★ *David Attenborough* ★ *Pamela Stephenson* ★ *Alec Guinness* ★
★ *Stevie Wonder* ★ *Elliott Gould* ★ *Germaine Greer* ★

The Tiger Year in Focus

ANCIENT WISDOM TELLS US that Tiger Years announce themselves with a roar. In this year we can expect conflict, devastation, international crises and political upheavals. Events occur suddenly, giving little warning of their profound impact; the majority of Tiger incidents will unleash trains of events whose consequences leave mankind reeling for years to come.

THE DARING AND THE BRAVE do much better in the Year of the Tiger than the meek and the timid. Grand schemes and extravagant gestures are the flavour of the day. For the impulsive, risks may backfire, but those with nerves of steel find the thrill of danger will sharpen their appetites and hone their claws.

EMOTIONALLY, it is a year for passion and intrigue, with sex rather than love high on the agenda. Should you be tempted to embark on an illicit fling, bear in mind the devastating repercussions of any action taken in the Year of the Tiger.

> ### ACTIVITIES ASSOCIATED
> ### WITH THE YEAR OF THE TIGER
> The discovery, invention, patenting, marketing or
> manufacturing of: dynamite, television, disk brakes,
> the vacuum cleaner, Edison's electric battery,
> the photocopier.

虎

40

Your Tiger Fortunes
for the Next 12 Years

1996 MARKS THE BEGINNING of a new 12-year cycle in the Chinese calendar. How your relationships and worldly prospects fare will depend on the influence of each Animal year in turn.

1996 YEAR OF THE RAT | *19 Feb 1996 – 6 Feb 1997*

The pacy nature of the Rat Year may incline you to take undue risks or to overstretch yourself and your resources. This is not a particularly lucky year for Tigers so watch your finances. Social and emotional life, however, fare a good deal better.

YEAR TREND: CONTROL YOUR SPENDING

1997 YEAR OF THE OX | *7 Feb 1997 – 27 Jan 1998*

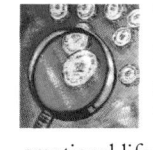

The slower pace and need for restraint required in an Oxen Year are not conducive to your fiery needs so 1997 could be frustrating. Emotionally and career-wise, this will be a year for overcoming obstacles.

YEAR TREND: MAINTAIN A LOW PROFILE

1998 YEAR OF THE TIGER | *28 Jan 1998 – 15 Feb 1999*

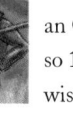

Most Tigers will be relieved to see the back of the Year of the Ox and give a cheer for 1998. You'll be more active this year and your prospects will improve dramatically, but do not throw all caution to the wind. Put something by for a rainy day.

YEAR TREND: A TIME TO SPREAD YOUR WINGS

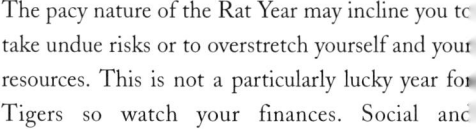

12 YEARS
OF TIGER
FORTUNES

虎

41

1999 YEAR OF THE RABBIT *16 Feb 1999 – 4 Feb 2000*

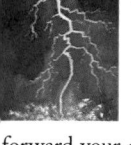

Last year's activity will continue to pay dividends for you now, so you'll feel lighter at heart and inclined to have some fun. Emotional life and love affairs bring much satisfaction.

YEAR TREND: **TAKE THINGS EASY**

2000 YEAR OF THE DRAGON *5 Feb 2000 – 23 Jan 2001*

Tigers get high on the electrically-charged atmosphere of Dragon Years so the first year of the new millennium promises to bring you excitement and a positive sense of challenge in which to push forward your objectives. Love will seek you out this year.

YEAR TREND: **HEADY**

The new millennium promises to be exciting and eventful

2001 YEAR OF THE SNAKE *24 Jan 2001 – 11 Feb 2002*

If there is one area of your life above all others that could give rise to problems this year it is your relationships. Dealings with relatives, colleagues and lovers may not be quite as straightforward as you would like and emotional entanglements could cost you dear.

YEAR TREND: **BEWARE DANGEROUS UNDERCURRENTS**

虎

42

2002 YEAR OF THE HORSE · *12 Feb 2002 – 31 Jan 2003*

This year your worldly aspirations take a quantum leap forward. Past efforts will be rewarded and a step up the ladder could boost your income. Passion is the name of the dating game among Tiger Lovers.

YEAR TREND: UPBEAT

2003 YEAR OF THE SHEEP · *1 Feb 2003 – 21 Jan 2004*

Although for you 2003 will lack a certain *pizzazz*, you can still make slow and steady progress in all areas of your life. For best effect, though, use this year as a period of rest and rehabilitation or treat it as a sabbatical away from your normal pressures.

YEAR TREND: LEARN THE MEANING OF TRANQUILLITY

2004 YEAR OF THE MONKEY · *22 Jan 2004 – 8 Feb 2005*

Despite some financial problems and the odd unexpected hurdle, there'll be plenty of scope and opportunities for you to make fair progress this year. Emotionally, it's a time for compromise since people and events will sorely try your patience.

YEAR TREND: WATCH OUT FOR GREMLINS

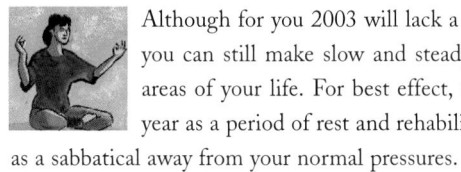

Look forward to a busy social life in 2005.

虎

2005 YEAR OF THE ROOSTER | *9 Feb 2005 – 28 Jan 2006*

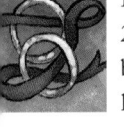

The auspices promise a buoyant and stimulating year. Your finances will be pleasing and your career should go well. You could achieve at least one of your major ambitions in 2005. Social life, too, will be busy and there'll be lots of happy comings and goings.

YEAR TREND: A TIME OF PROSPERITY AND WELL-BEING

2006 YEAR OF THE DOG | *29 Jan 2006 – 17 Feb 2007*

Domestically stable and romantically uplifting, in 2006 friends, colleagues and relations will bend over backwards to smooth your path. This year promises happiness if you put down roots or tie the knot.

YEAR TREND: A MOST SATISFYING YEAR

2007 YEAR OF THE PIG | *18 Feb 2007 – 6 Feb 2008*

Keep your eyes open throughout 2007 for any opportunities that come your way and be sure you're in a position to grab them. This is not a year for hiding your light under a bushel; you must promote yourself if you want to succeed. Romance is steady.

YEAR TREND: GO FOR IT